DRESSING UP FOR HALLOWEEN

By Cliff Griswold

Gareth Stevens
PUBLISHING

Please visit our website, www.garethstevens.com. For a free color catalog of all our high-quality books, call toll free 1-800-542-2595 or fax 1-877-542-2596.

Library of Congress Cataloging-in-Publication Data

Griswold, Cliff.
Dressing up for Halloween / by Cliff Griswold.
p. cm. — (Fun in fall)
Includes index.
ISBN 978-1-4824-1773-9 (pbk.)
ISBN 978-1-4824-1774-6 (6-pack)
ISBN 978-1-4824-1772-2 (library binding)
1. Halloween — Juvenile literature. I. Griswold, Cliff. II. Title.
GT4965.G75 2015
394.2646 —d23

First Edition

Published in 2015 by
Gareth Stevens Publishing
111 East 14th Street, Suite 349
New York, NY 10003

Editor: Ryan Nagelhout
Designer: Nicholas Domiano

Photo credits: Cover, p.1 KidStock/Blend Images/Getty Images; p. 5 Vstock LLC/Getty Images; pp. 7, 11, 13, 19, 21, 23, 24 (pumpkin, witch) Monkey Business Images/Shutterstock.com; p. 9 wavebreakmedia/Shutterstock.com; p. 15 WilleeCole Photography/Shutterstock.com; p. 17 © iStockphoto.com/kali9.

Printed in the United States of America

CPSIA compliance information: Batch #CW15GS: For further information contact Gareth Stevens, New York, New York at 1-800-542-2595.

Contents

It is October 31.
Today is Halloween!

I love to dress up.

My mom made
my outfit.

I look like a witch.

My friends wear
outfits, too.

Even my dog Spot dressed up. She looks like a pumpkin.

We go trick-or-treating!

We go to many houses.
We got lots of candy.

My sister Sara put it in a pumpkin.

Later we go
to a Halloween party.

Words to Know

pumpkin

witch

Index

24